Tim

Bapt

Text copyright © Brian Sears 2014
The author asserts the moral right
to be identified as the author of this work

Published by
The Bible Reading Fellowship
15 The Chambers, Vineyard
Abingdon OX14 3FE
United Kingdom
Tel: +44 (0)1865 319700
Email: enquiries@brf.org.uk
Website: www.brf.org.uk
BRF is a Registered Charity

ISBN 978 0 85746 154 4

First published 2014
10 9 8 7 6 5 4 3 2 1
All rights reserved

Acknowledgments
Unless otherwise stated, scripture quotations are taken from the Contemporary English Version of the Bible published by HarperCollins Publishers, copyright © 1991, 1992, 1995 American Bible Society.

Cover illustration: Maria Maddocks/The Organisation

A catalogue record for this book is available from the British Library

Printed and bound by CPI Group (UK) Ltd, Croydon CR0 4YY

Timothy Bear
and the
Baptism Box

12 five-minute stories and simple activities
for baptism families

Brian Sears

To our grandchildren

Preface: The world of Timothy Bear

Timothy Bear's world consists mainly of his home, his school and his church. His parents, Mr and Mrs Bear, seek the very best for Timothy and his sister Teresa. Teresa is generally helpful to her brother but sometimes she can be a pain—as he can be to her! Grandma and Grandpa are very important figures in Timothy's and Teresa's lives. It's probably true to say that Grandpa is the last person on earth that Timothy would want to upset.

Timothy Bear attends the local primary school, which takes children and bears from nursery until it's time to move on to secondary school. Stories in other *Timothy Bear* books have concentrated on his school life but here the emphasis is on home and church, although the world of school is not entirely neglected and appears at appropriate places. Timothy's family attend their local church, and Timothy enjoys his time there. He learns about a God who is interested in everything about him; he learns about Jesus, who shows us what God is like; and he learns about the Bible, a book full of wonderful stories. Gradually the happenings in his life help him to understand how this all fits in, not only at church but also at school, at home and in the whole of Timothy Bear's world.

Contents

Foreword 8

Introduction 9

Telling Timothy Bear stories to children 11

1 Timothy Bear to the rescue.. 13

2 Timothy changes direction 19

3 Built on the rock.. 27

4 Water! 33

5 Three in one 39

6 The anointing oil 45

7 Don't touch the trifle! 51

8 Promises, promises 57

9 Light of Teresa's life 63

10 Serving others.. 67

11 Pirates ahoy! 73

12 If a job's worth doing.. 79

Foreword

Baptism is the beginning of a journey we make in the Christian life, welcomed into the Christian family and guided by others in the footsteps of faith. Often we are baptised as young babies and it is an event, although a very important one, that we know nothing about.

It is not always easy to explain to young children what baptism really means, and as a vicar I am often asked to teach the RE lessons on baptism at the local primary school as well as to prepare families for baptism. Often we re-enact the process with a doll, but it can be hard to explain all the elements and symbols. So it is great to have a book to recommend, which can be read to young children with activities to involve children and parents alike.

Through twelve simple stories, *Timothy Bear and the Baptism Box* takes you on a journey as Timothy Bear witnesses his sister Teresa's baptism and gets to ask questions about the themes and symbols associated with baptism.

The book is primarily written for children, but parents, clergy and teachers would all benefit from its child-centred explanations of the symbols of baptism and the themes woven through the Christian story around it.

My favourite part of the book is the Baptism Box itself—the making of a memory box that helps children to make a tangible connection with their baptism while having fun.

Revd Jane Hemmings, Rector of the Akeman Benefice

Introduction

Timothy Bear and the Baptism Box takes as its starting point the Church of England service of infant baptism. Themes from that service are woven into the stories. The stories become a way for children to understand more of what infant baptism means. Most children will be much too young even to remember their own service, but this book is a way for them and their families to reflect on the event and what it means and goes on meaning.

Timothy's family identify with church life and are part of its ministry and fellowship. Timothy's grandparents and godparents are very important to him. Water is the vital ingredient of baptism and it splashes up in several of the stories. Oil and a candle can also be part of infant baptism, and there are stories to explore why this is so. Spiritual themes are illustrated—repentance, forgiveness through the sacrifice of Jesus, growing as a Christian, keeping promises, service and perseverance.

I hope that each story will have a positive impact just through its telling or reading. Children may well add their own comments or questions, which will provide natural follow-up. Gentle adult questioning may be in order, too. Adult help in the activity suggestions is important. The basis of that is the provision of a suitable 'Baptism Box' so that this book can become a memorable experience in the lives of our children.

Telling Timothy Bear stories to children

In the telling of these stories, the presence of a teddy bear must be helpful! Timothy Bear is delighted when his name is adopted by other bears, but he also understands if his name in the stories has to be changed to that of a different bear. Many families will produce their own brand of stories to mirror events in their own family lives.

I am not gifted in the ability to produce a range of voices and accents, but even I can manage a deep, gruff voice for anything said by Timothy. Children seem to enjoy listening out for such input. Families are encouraged to add local colour to their storytelling; we used to have a local Reverend Walker who often became 'Reverend Corker'!

— Chapter 1 —

Timothy Bear to the rescue

Timothy turns out to be an important part of his sister's baptism day. He makes a Baptism Box and places a nameplate with Teresa's name inside. The storyline follows the events of the baptism service. Because of his interest in shells, Timothy has spotted where the minister has mislaid his scallop shell and comes to the rescue.

What the minister said

'Welcome to our service today—and a special welcome to Teresa Bear and her family on the day of her baptism.'

Story preamble

The vicar can't find a vital item… but Timothy, because of his interest in shells, saves the day… and after the service makes a copy of his sister's name to put in his Baptism Box.

Bible verses

Some people brought their children to Jesus so that he could bless them by placing his hands on them. But his disciples told the people to stop bothering him. When Jesus saw this, he became angry and said, 'Let the children come to me! Don't try to stop them. People who are like these little children belong to the kingdom of God. I promise you that you cannot get into God's

kingdom, unless you accept it the way a child does.' Then Jesus took the children in his arms and blessed them by placing his hands on them.
MARK 10:13–16

TIMOTHY BEAR TO THE RESCUE

Timothy Bear had been interested in shells for a long time. Whenever he was at the seaside he would search the shore for shells. Grandma even taught Timothy a tongue-twister that she learned when she was a girl: 'She sells seashells by the seashore.' Timothy would sometimes say it to himself as he was adding to his collection of special shells.

At home, Timothy added to his knowledge of shells by looking them up in books and on the internet. He learned to recognise lots of different kinds—cockles and mussels, periwinkles, limpets and razor shells. Little did Timothy realise how important his knowledge of shells would be at Teresa's baptism.

The Bear family and, indeed, the whole church had been looking forward to the occasion of Teresa's baptism for a long time. It would take place as part of the morning service. To add to the excitement, it happened to be the day of Teresa's first birthday—a double celebration! Afterwards there would be a special lunch at the church and then the family would return home for a birthday party. What a day! Timothy would especially enjoy all the food.

The Bear family arrived at church in good time. They were greeted with lots of smiles. Teresa, especially, was much admired. Timothy wandered to the back of the church, where there was a special area reserved for children and cubs, with books and toys. He walked past the font, around which, he knew, he and his family would gather when it came to Teresa's baptism. Just beyond the font, Timothy glanced at the table of magazines, books and postcards for people to buy. There, in the middle of the table, he was amazed to find one of the biggest shells he had ever seen. It was as big as a saucer! Timothy remembered seeing a picture of one just like it in a book; he was sure its name began with 'S'.

When Timothy rejoined his family, it was time for the service to begin. It was indeed a joyful, happy service, and the vicar led it carefully and caringly. It was soon time for Teresa's baptism. The vicar invited the Bear family and godparents to join him and his curate round the font. When they were all in position, Timothy noticed that the vicar was looking a little worried.

Timothy was near enough to hear the vicar whisper to his curate, 'Oh dear! I've forgotten where I put my scallop shell for scooping up the baptism water. I'm sure I brought it with me.'

Suddenly, Timothy remembered the name of the shell he had seen. *Of course! Scallop!*

'I know where it is,' whispered Timothy to the vicar. 'I'll get it.'

Delighted, the vicar watched Timothy walk across to the table and carefully bring back the precious scallop shell. The vicar was back to his comfortable, jovial self. He patted Timothy's head.

'Teresa is a fortunate sister to have Timothy for her brother—and he certainly knows his shells!'

Timothy followed his sister's baptism with much interest. He imagined what it must have been like for him when he had been baptised as a baby cub. He especially liked the part when the vicar scooped up the water in the scallop shell and splashed it over Teresa's head. Timothy remembered how Teresa had hated having a bath when she was newly born. Now, although she was not full of smiles, she did not cry either. Perhaps somehow she knew how special this time was for her. Timothy was so proud of his sister.

The rest of the service and Teresa's birthday passed in a pleasant glow. Finally, it was time for Timothy to go up to bed. He got out his Baptism Box, which would help to remind him of such a special time and special people. Before he went to sleep, he wrote Teresa's name on a piece of paper and surrounded it with carefully drawn scallop shells. The last thing he did was to place the paper inside his Baptism Box. It had indeed been a day to remember.

Activity

With the help of your family, find a suitable box to become your Baptism Box. A shoe box (or shoe box size) would be ideal. The outside of the box could be decorated over time. As well as being a Baptism Box, it could have a wider purpose—to hold a collection of childhood memories.

Make a nameplate for a baby or a friend whose baptism you have attended or plan to attend. Place the nameplate in your Baptism Box as a reminder to pray for the person who has been baptised.

Prayer

Lord Jesus, you welcomed children to come to you when you were on earth. You go on welcoming us when we come to you through your church. In our turn, help us to be welcoming to others. Amen.

✣

— Chapter 2 —

Timothy changes direction

Timothy learns that to 'repent' means to turn and face the right direction. Mr Bear tells a story from the Bible about how Jesus is that right direction.

What the minister said

'On the day of Pentecost, Peter said, "Repent and be baptised, every one of you, in the name of Jesus Christ, so that your sins may be forgiven." This verse from Acts 2:38 shows us that repentance and baptism go together.'

Story preamble

Timothy learns that to 'repent' means to turn and face the right direction… and Mr Bear tells a seaside Bible story about Jesus being and showing that right direction.

Bible verses

Simon Peter said, 'I'm going fishing!' The others said, 'We will go with you.' They went out in their boat. But they didn't catch a thing that night. Early the next morning Jesus stood on the shore, but the disciples did not realise who he was. Jesus shouted, 'Friends, have you caught anything?' 'No!' they answered. So he told them, 'Let your net down on the right side of your boat, and you will catch some fish.' They did, and the net was so full of

fish that they could not drag it up into the boat. Jesus' favourite disciple told Peter, 'It's the Lord!' When Simon heard that it was the Lord, he put on the clothes that he had taken off while he was working. Then he jumped into the water. The boat was only about a hundred metres from shore. So the other disciples stayed in the boat and dragged in the net full of fish.
JOHN 21:3–8

TIMOTHY CHANGES DIRECTION

It was a few days before Teresa's baptism. By the end of the day, Timothy Bear thought his mum must have been right when she'd said, 'Whatever's up with you, Timothy? You must have got out of bed on the wrong side!'

She said it first of all at breakfast, when Timothy arrived in the kitchen all cross and grumbling. His pullover was on back-to-front as well. Dad tried to make a joke about it: 'Either he'll have to take it off and put it on the right way round or we'll have to twist his head round the other way!'

I'm afraid that Timothy rudely stuck his tongue out. It was then that Mrs Bear mentioned wrong sides of beds. Timothy realised it must just be one of Mum's sayings, as his bed is right up against the wall and there's only one way to get out of it.

At school, Miss Read had her class playing 'Simon says' as a warm-up for their PE lesson.

'Simon says: "Face the front!"' Miss Read announced. Her whole class stood smartly facing their teacher.

'Turn around!' called Miss Read.

Obediently, Timothy jumped to face in the opposite direction—but he was the only one to move.

'Oh dear, Timothy! Only when "Simon says". You're looking in quite the wrong direction. Come here and help me look for the next cub to be caught out.'

Timothy supposed it was all part of 'getting out of bed on the wrong side'.

In the next lesson, Timothy was caught out much more

seriously looking in the wrong direction. They were doing number work. Miss Read had been working hard with her class, adding 5 to a whole range of numbers. Timothy had been daydreaming during the lesson, and now Miss Read was giving a test to see how well her class were doing.

Timothy found the questions impossibly hard. However, he was sitting next to Penny, who had been paying attention in class—and she could add 5 to any number quickly and confidently. Timothy's eyes wandered to Penny's neatly written answers. It would be so easy to transfer them to his page.

'Timothy!' Miss Read was using her sharp voice. 'You're facing the wrong way again. Keep your eyes on your own work.'

Timothy's day did not improve. At lunch time, he accidently bumped into Linda and knocked her over. Instead of making sure she was all right, Timothy just carried on carelessly careering round the playground. While Mrs Sullivan was looking after Linda, she heard how the accident had happened. Then she went to find Timothy.

'It's not like you, Timothy,' pointed out Mrs Sullivan. 'Usually you look out for others, but today you're only thinking about yourself. You need to change direction!'

For once, Timothy was glad when his school day was over. However, his troublesome day hadn't ended. Mrs Bear had a reminder for him.

'Timothy, you need to reply to that invitation.'

Timothy had been invited to a Teddy Bears' picnic.

'When is it?' asked Timothy.

Timothy changes direction

'You'll have to find the invitation,' replied Mum.

Could he find it? He looked in all the likely places, and then he looked in all the *unlikely* places—some of them more than once. He even suggested that his mum must have put it somewhere impossible to find. In the end, Mr Bear announced that it was bedtime.

'Five minutes to read your book and then I've time to tell you a story—a Bible story tonight.'

Timothy almost stamped upstairs. What a day! How many times had he been looking in the wrong direction? He hardly felt like reading. Bad-tempered, he grabbed his reading book and flung it open. Out fell the Teddy Bears' picnic invitation! He had used it to mark his place the night before.

Mr Bear's Bible story was about seven men who went fishing all night but didn't manage to catch anything, not a single bite. Their net remained empty. As the sun came up, they rowed their boat towards the shore. Then, a person called out to them from the beach.

'Throw your net to starboard!' shouted the stranger on the shore.

'You see,' said Mr Bear to Timothy, 'the fishermen had been looking in the wrong direction.'

'I know the feeling,' said Timothy, remembering his breakfast, the game of 'Simon says', the number test, poor Linda in the playground and the lost invitation.

Dad went on to complete the story: the person on the shore was Jesus; the early morning catch of fish in the end numbered 153; and they made a delicious breakfast on the beach. The story cheered Timothy Bear. He would begin to look in the directions that Jesus wanted, and tomorrow morning he'd be sure to get out of his bed on the right side!

Activity

Early Christians used a simple sketch of a fish as a secret sign to each other. You might find a badge or a brooch in the shape of a fish to keep, perhaps in your Baptism Box. You could also make your own fish picture—maybe a picture from the Bible story that Mr Bear told Timothy at bedtime.

Prayer

Lord Jesus, forgive us when we turn away from what is good and turn away from you. Turn us back, and help us to walk in your ways. Amen

— Chapter 3 —

Built on the rock

Timothy and his family come to the front of the church with Teresa's godparents. The minister asks the baptism questions. Then he makes the sign of the cross on Teresa's forehead; Mr Bear, Mrs Bear and Timothy do the same. Before they move to the font, Timothy hears a story about rock and sand. He remembers his own 'rock and sand' story and thinks about what the story teaches us for our own lives.

What the minister said

'I invite Mr and Mrs Bear, Timothy and Teresa to come to the front, and the godparents to join us.'

Story preamble

Uncle Ian, Teresa's godfather, arranges an outing... Timothy encounters two castles... and determines to build his life on the rock.

Bible verses

Anyone who hears and obeys these teachings of mine is like a wise person who built a house on solid rock. Rain poured down, rivers flooded, and winds beat against that house. But it did not fall, because it was built on solid rock. Anyone who hears my teachings and doesn't obey them is like a foolish person who built a house

on sand. The rain poured down, the rivers flooded, and the winds blew and beat against that house. Finally, it fell with a crash.
MATTHEW 7:24–27

BUILT ON THE ROCK

Uncle Ian and Auntie Catherine are Timothy's godparents. The only trouble is that they live about 100 miles away. Uncle Ian does what he can to keep in touch. He always remembers Timothy on his birthday and at Christmas. There are occasional visits. Uncle Ian is also good at sending letters and postcards. As a godparent, he remembers to help Timothy in his thinking about God and about what Jesus means to the world, the church and to Timothy.

Timothy was excited when the most recent postcard arrived. It had been agreed that Timothy was old enough to go to stay with Uncle Ian and Auntie Catherine for a few days at half-term. The invitation to do so was on the postcard.

'It says Uncle Ian is going to take me to the seaside to visit the castle that's on the card,' announced Timothy, pointing at the picture of a splendid ancient castle.

'It may have been knocked about a bit over the centuries,' warned Dad.

Half-term soon came. Uncle Ian and Timothy went by train to visit the seaside and its castle. They saw the castle from the train window.

'It doesn't look too knocked about,' said Timothy.

'We'll visit it this afternoon,' decided Uncle Ian. 'This morning, while the sun is out, we'll go to the beach.'

Uncle Ian and Timothy agreed that they would make a huge sandcastle by the water's edge. It grew and took shape remarkably quickly. It was easily the biggest sandcastle on the beach. They dug out a deep moat all the way round their castle. Timothy was delighted with their efforts. He was just about to bring bucketsful of water for the moat when the incoming tide began to do the job for him. It was all working out so well!

'Time for us to eat our packed lunch,' said Uncle Ian.

They did just that, sitting on a handy breakwater. However, by the time they had reached the honey tarts in the superb packed lunch, the moat of their castle was full to overflowing and bits of the castle were being undermined and slipping into the water.

'Oh no,' moaned Timothy, realising that their morning's work was being undone. 'All our efforts wasted!'

Uncle Ian smiled.

'Not quite, Timothy,' he said quietly. 'Jesus told us a story about wise and foolish building. Anything built on sand soon gets washed away, and it's easy to knock it down. If we foolishly leave Jesus and God out of our thinking and out of our living, it's like building on sand.'

It was a long speech for Uncle Ian to make, and he hadn't quite finished.

'And now we'll visit that castle up there. It was built nearly one thousand years ago.'

'One thousand!' gasped Timothy.

It was quite a climb to reach the castle. You could see and feel the rock that the castle had been built on. When they reached the drawbridge that allowed them to cross the ancient moat, it was quite windy. As Timothy's dad had said, the castle had been 'knocked about a bit over the centuries' by the wind and weather and by invaders trying to get in.

However, you could still see the pattern of rooms and how it had been lived in hundreds of years before.

Uncle Ian bought ice creams and they sat in the shelter of the Great Hall.

'What a difference it makes when you build a castle on rock,' Timothy exclaimed thoughtfully. He was remembering how swiftly their own sandcastle had been demolished by the waves of the incoming tide.

'That's right,' replied Uncle Ian. 'Sometimes the Bible compares God to a safe place, like a castle, and sometimes God is like the rock. In the story we were thinking about on the beach, Jesus said that building our lives on his words and his ways is like building on rock.'

'That's what I mean to do all my life,' said Timothy, crunching the last of his cone.

Activity

Fold a piece of paper in half from the top to the bottom. On the left-hand side, draw a castle on a rock. Give it the title 'Build on the rock'. On the right-hand side, draw a sandcastle being knocked down by the incoming tide. Give that one the title 'Don't build on the sand'.

You could also keep in your Baptism Box something (perhaps a postcard) to remind you of a special day out.

Prayer

God, our Heavenly Father, thank you for the strength we find in you. Help us to build our lives on your words and your ways. Amen

— Chapter 4 —

Water!

Timothy realises the difference that water makes in the sea, the river and the bath; Grandpa talks about the importance of water in our lives; and Timothy remembers how the vicar poured water on Teresa's head at her baptism. Grandpa goes on to explain how, in baptism, water is a sign of being washed free from the things we do wrong and beginning a new life with God. Grandpa describes what his own baptism still means to him, and Timothy goes to sleep feeling clean outside and in.

What the minister said

'We are now going to move to the font so that we can baptise Teresa with water. All the children who are with us today are invited to gather round so that they can see.'

Story preamble

Timothy realises the difference water makes in the sea, in the river and in the bath… Grandpa talks about why water is used in baptism… and Timothy goes to sleep feeling clean inside as well as outside.

Bible verse

Baptism is more than just washing your body. It means turning to God with a clear conscience, because Jesus Christ was raised from death.
1 PETER 3:21

WATER!

The Bear family was on holiday with Grandma and Grandpa. It had been agreed that Timothy and Grandpa should have the whole day to themselves on Tuesday. When Tuesday arrived, Grandpa gently shook Timothy awake early.

'Come on, young cub,' urged Grandpa. 'We're spending this morning on the beach, and I've got permission to take you swimming in the sea.'

Timothy smiled. He was getting used to the surprising things that Grandpa often had in store for him. He had had a course of lessons in the swimming pool back home, but he'd never been in the sea before.

Grandpa and Timothy were so early that there was no problem parking the car, and the beach was almost deserted. The sun was already quite high in the sky and the sea sparkled in its rays.

'Best to swim first, then we'll do things on the beach to dry off,' said Grandpa.

How cold the water felt to start with! But grandpa and grandcub soon got used to it. Timothy hadn't yet learned to swim properly in the pool back home. However, in the sea, with Grandpa and the salty water both supporting him, he even floated on his own once or twice. It was great fun, and so refreshing. Timothy tingled with life.

'A good swim always sets me up for the day,' commented Grandpa when he thought it was time to come out of the sea and back to the beach. There were so many things to do on the beach, and their bodies gradually dried in the sunshine. Timothy still tingled.

Water!

Grandpa had heard the weather forecast, so he knew it was likely that clouds would roll in from the west. That was why he had woken Timothy early and had already made plans to go from the seaside into the nearby forest for the afternoon.

'We'll find a river and see if we can catch some fish,' said Grandpa, still surprising Timothy. A fishing expedition would be another new experience for Timothy Bear. Excitement mingled with the tingle he was still feeling from his early morning swim.

At the handy table near the river, grandpa and grandcub ate the picnic that Grandma had packed for them. Then Grandpa revealed the fishing nets and bucket he had stored in the boot of the car. He reckoned cloud cover would increase their chances of catching fish, but he told Timothy right from the start that they would return any fish they caught to their watery home. Timothy saw the sense of that.

Fishing was hard but enjoyable work and required much patience. The river was shallow and very muddy; Grandpa was much better than Timothy at keeping himself clean.

Time just flew by. It didn't seem long before Grandpa announced that it was time to go back and join the others.

'I'll empty the bucket,' said the mud-spattered Timothy, and he picked up the bucket of fish they had caught.

He thought it would be best to empty it near the middle of the river. As he returned to Grandpa, he looked over his shoulder to check that the fish were getting used to the water again. It was then that he tripped over a tree-root growing out from the bank. He stumbled full-length into the mud. What a shock! What a mess! Grandpa bent to lift up the bedraggled Timothy, and Grandpa's smile soon spread to Timothy's face as well.

'Let's get you home as soon as we can!' said Grandpa, leading Timothy to the car and opening the door. 'Here, sit on this towel while I drive, and then we'll put you straight into the bath.'

Grandma held up her paws in mock horror when she saw Timothy. The smell wasn't too pleasant either. The others all agreed that—as it was still their day to themselves—Grandpa should have the task of cleaning up his grandcub. A lot of rubbing, scrubbing and rub-a-dub-dubbing went on in the bath. Eventually, Timothy emerged as his normal, cleansed and sweet-smelling self.

'I'm still tingling,' sighed Timothy as Grandpa tucked him up in his bed.

Grandpa had got into the habit, on holiday, of giving Timothy something to think about at the end of each day. It must have been all the water in this day—the sea in the morning, the river with its fish and mud in the afternoon, and now the bath in the evening—that prompted Grandpa to be thinking of baptism.

Grandpa started to talk about the importance of water in our lives. As he did so, Timothy reminded him how the vicar had poured water on Teresa's head at her baptism. Grandpa explained how, in baptism, water is a sign of being washed free from the things we do wrong and beginning a new life with God.

'Like you, Timothy, I was much too young to remember being baptised,' began Grandpa, 'but I think about it a lot.

It makes me tingle even when I haven't been in the sea. And remember—although water can only clean our outsides, what Jesus goes on doing for us is cleaning our insides too.'

Timothy thought back over his day and smiled at what Grandpa was saying.

'I feel fresh and clean all over, inside and out,' murmured Timothy, already half-asleep.

Activity

Make a list with someone of the many ways that water is useful to us. Place the list in your Baptism Box and use it as a way of saying 'thank you' to God in quiet moments of the day.

Prayer

Lord Jesus, we thank you for the water of baptism. We thank you that water reminds us of growth, refreshment and being clean. We thank you that water speaks to us of our life in you. Amen

Chapter 5

Three in one

One day, Timothy's neighbour Mrs Bradman is taken ill and has to go into a care home. Timothy helps Mr and Mrs Bear by visiting Mrs Bradman while she is getting better until, one day, she is well enough to go back to her own home.

What the minister said

'Teresa, I baptise you in the name of the Father, and of the Son, and of the Holy Spirit.'

Story preamble

The minister talks about Jesus' baptism… wonders if the Bear family can help Mrs Bradman… and gets another example of three working as one.

Bible verses

About that time Jesus came from Nazareth in Galilee, and John baptised him in the River Jordan. As soon as Jesus came out of the water, he saw the sky open and the Holy Spirit coming down to him like a dove. A voice from heaven said, 'You are my own dear Son, and I am pleased with you.'
MARK 1:9–11

THREE IN ONE

At church, the vicar was doing a series of services to help his congregation understand baptism. One service, of course, was all about Jesus being baptised in the River Jordan. The vicar pointed out that it is a wonderful example of God the Father, God the Son and God the Holy Spirit working together in perfect harmony. As John the Baptist was baptising Jesus, God the Father's voice was heard saying, 'You are my own dear Son, and I am pleased with you.' As Jesus came up out of the river, the Spirit of God came in the form of a dove, flying down and resting on Jesus.

'Father and Spirit are one with the Son,' pointed out the vicar.

After the service, the vicar spoke to Mr Bear about Mrs Bradman.

'She's recovering quite well from her stroke,' he reported, 'but she's still very confused. They're moving her to a care home and I'm wondering if you and your family would go on keeping an eye on her.'

The vicar knew that Mr and Mrs Bear had been friends with Mrs Bradman for a long time, especially since her husband had died.

Mr Bear smiled. 'We'll do what we can, but having a young baby around takes up quite a bit of our time.'

So it was that Mr Bear passed on the vicar's wishes to Mum and Timothy. 'Why don't you two go and visit Mrs Bradman in the care home?' suggested Dad. 'I'll look after Teresa.' It was agreed, and the visit was arranged.

Mrs Bradman did not appear to recognise her two visitors at all. She wasn't even wearing her glasses, and her eyes looked blank.

'What have you had for dinner?' asked Mrs Bear.

'Baked beans and custard,' said the unsmiling Mrs Bradman.

'What, together?' blurted out Timothy.

Mrs Bradman nodded.

'And what about visitors?' asked Mrs Bear.

'I'm waiting for Mr Bradman to come,' said the still unsmiling Mrs Bradman.

Timothy was not even old enough to remember Mr Bradman being alive.

'Things are bad,' said Mum quietly to Timothy. 'You wait with Mrs B while I go to find a carer to get some advice.'

Timothy felt quite at ease sitting with Mrs Bradman. He'd had such good times with her in the past, and he longed to help her back to her normal self again. Mrs B certainly couldn't remember much about her recent past, but what about the distant past? Timothy thought about the nursery rhymes he knew and loved; perhaps Mrs B had also learned them as a child.

'Half a pound of tuppenny rice,' began Timothy slowly, 'half a pound of treacle. That's the way the money goes…'

But before Timothy could go on, 'Pop!' was uttered by Mrs Bradman, and for the first time a smile flickered across her face.

Encouraged, Timothy realised he might be on the right track, so next he took Mrs Bradman's hand in his paw. With his other paw, he began to make circles on her hand.

'Round and round the garden like a teddy bear. One step, two steps…'

Timothy paused and was delighted to hear Mrs Bradman making giggling sounds in anticipation of the coming tickles.

As those tickles were being delivered, Mrs Bear returned. She was amazed at the turn of events.

'I must find my glasses,' Mrs Bradman was saying. 'I do believe my visitor is a bear called Timothy.'

The vicar later reported that the care home thought Mrs Bradman's return to normal health began with that afternoon's visit. It developed through several other visits until Mrs B was well enough to return to her own home. The vicar thanked Mr Bear.

'I only set it in motion,' protested Mr Bear. 'It was all three of us working together,' he went on.

'An example of a trinity of bears working as one!' smiled the vicar, pleased with himself.

Activity

Draw three triangles on a piece of card and cut them out. On the corners of one of the triangles, write Mum, Dad and Timothy; on the corners of the second triangle, write Father, Son and Holy Spirit; and on the corners of the third, write your own name and two others that would make a triangle of help. Place the three triangles in your Baptism Box and use them to remind you about the help that each member of the Trinity—Father, Son and Holy Spirit—gives us.

Prayer

Heavenly Father, thank you for our wonderful world; Lord Jesus, thank you that you love our world so much; Holy Spirit, thank you for being at work for good in our world. Amen

— Chapter 6 —

The anointing oil

Timothy learns that being part of a family can be joyful even when things don't seem to be going right.

What the minister said

'May God, who has received you by baptism into his Church, pour upon you the riches of his grace.'

Story preamble

Mrs Bear and Timothy prepare themselves for sports day… are both disappointed not to win… but then take part in the shopping bags marathon.

Bible verses

It is truly wonderful when relatives live together in peace. It is as beautiful as olive oil poured on Aaron's head and running down his beard and the collar of his robe. It is like the dew from Mount Hermon, falling on Zion's mountains, where the Lord has promised to bless his people with life for evermore.
PSALM 133

THE ANOINTING OIL

Timothy Bear took in every detail of Teresa's baptism. He noticed that, after Teresa's baptism with water, the vicar made the sign of the cross on his sister's head with some oil that had a wonderful smell. In the excitement of all that happened on the day, Timothy forgot to ask about the oil.

It was only when Mum was getting Timothy ready for his school's sports day, months later, that he remembered. It was because Mum was rubbing his joints with some oil, and its smell reminded Timothy of Teresa's baptism.

'I'm doing this for you today, Timothy,' explained Mrs Bear, 'to help your muscles to run your races more smoothly. The vicar did it for Teresa so that God might go on using her to do the things he wants her to do; you had the same done for you when you were baptised. God wants you to go on living his way every day—sports day included.' Mrs Bear smiled. She didn't usually make such long speeches.

Timothy had understood. 'So this oil is especially for sports day, but that oil in church is to help me do good and right things every day?'

Mum nodded. How good that Timothy was taking in things so well! Timothy noticed that Mum rubbed oil on herself as well.

'I'm going in for the mums' race,' she said.

Timothy knew he would be no good at the shorter races—he eats too much honey—but he was pinning his hopes on winning the mini-marathon, which always completed the events of sports day. By the time Timothy was lining up for that final race, Mrs Bear had already finished second in the mums' race. Timothy hoped to go one better.

As he started the mini-marathon, Timothy knew he mustn't set off too fast; he must keep something in reserve. But he found himself in front, and no one seemed to be keeping up with him. He heard his name being chanted across the field. 'Tim-oth-y, Tim-oth-y!'

Then the race track took the runners behind the school, away from the spectators. Just as he was emerging into the supporters' sight again, Timothy was conscious of the beat of feet on the ground behind him. Another name was being chanted with his own. 'Ell-ie, Ell-ie, Ell-ie!'

He had a race on his paws after all! Timothy just kept his lead into the finishing straight. However, the slight upward slope of the final 50 metres proved too much for him. Ellie had paced herself just a little bit better, and she swept ahead in the final strides.

Sports day was over!

The disappointed Timothy met up with his mum. 'That oil didn't do much good,' he groaned.

'Well,' said Mum, 'without it we might have come further back than second. No kind of oil can make sure you win!'

On the way home, Timothy and Mrs Bear caught up with Mrs Garland, who was struggling home with her bags of shopping. Mrs Garland was an elderly lady from church and lived in the same road as the Bears. Timothy knew immediately what he should do. Putting the disappointment of the afternoon to one side, he offered to carry some of Mrs Garland's shopping.

Mum followed Timothy's lead. They ended up taking the bags right into Mrs Garland's kitchen. On the way, Mrs Garland asked what all the cheering had been about on the school field. Timothy explained about sports day—and about the disappointment of mother and cub on coming second.

When Mrs Garland saw that they had carefully placed all the shopping on her kitchen table, she put up her hand.

'I'm about to make a speech!' she announced. 'You may not have quite won your school races, but you've certainly come first in the shopping bags marathon. And I know which I think is more important!'

Timothy and his mum smiled their thanks. Mum was pleased to think, too, that Timothy's oil of baptism was continuing to be a sign of the right and good things he was doing in his life.

The anointing oil

Activity

Find a small, screw-topped jar and wash it thoroughly. Fill it with some olive oil and add a few drops of lavender oil. Place the top on the jar and shake it thoroughly. To make a pretty cover, cut out a circle of paper twice the diameter of the lid, decorate it with coloured crayons and fix it to the top of the jar with a strong rubber band. Keep the jar by the bath so that a few drops can be added to the water when you or a family member takes a bath.

For your Baptism Box, make a shopping list of items you would enjoy buying from a supermarket. Use that list as a 'thank you' prayer to God for some of the things he provides us with.

Prayer

Lord Jesus, thank you that you call us to serve you in our world. Strengthen us for the tasks you give us. We are sorry when we let you down. Amen

— Chapter 7 —

Don't touch the trifle!

One day, after Timothy has been particularly naughty, he sees a shadow made by his own body on the wall. Feeling sorry for his naughtiness, he finds that the shadow becomes a reminder and a comfort as he thinks about the action of signing the cross and the vicar's words at Teresa's baptism.

What the minister said

'Christ claims you for his own. Receive the sign of his cross.'

Story preamble

Timothy doesn't do as he's told… is very sorry… and finds that a shadow on the wall acts as a reminder and a comfort.

Bible verses

God rescued us from the dark power of Satan and brought us into the kingdom of his dear Son, who forgives our sins and sets us free.
COLOSSIANS 1:13–14

DON'T TOUCH THE TRIFLE!

It was a couple of days before Teresa's baptism. Mrs Bear was busy with preparations for the family and friends who would be coming. She had lots of shopping to do. Mum would take Teresa with her, and Timothy said he'd be quite all right by himself.

'We won't be long,' Mum said. 'Make sure you don't touch the trifle!'

Timothy had watched Mum make one of her special trifles that morning. It had fruit at the bottom, sponge on top of the fruit, jelly on top of the sponge, and pink blancmange on top of the jelly. Mum had put the special trifle in the fridge. It was for Teresa's party after her baptism.

Timothy found it strange being in the house on his own. He couldn't think what to do. He wandered upstairs to his bedroom. Then he wandered downstairs again. Perhaps he was feeling hungry. He found himself in the kitchen.

'Don't touch the trifle!' Mum's voice echoed inside his head. He certainly wouldn't touch the trifle but perhaps he ought to make sure it was safe inside the fridge. He would like a closer look. Mum hadn't said not to touch the *bowl* of the trifle!

Timothy lifted the bowl out of the fridge and on to the kitchen table. He noticed that the blancmange was a long way from setting—it flowed a little from side to side. Now he really did feel hungry.

Suddenly, Timothy had an idea. He fetched a spoon from the drawer and carefully removed a spoonful of pink

Don't touch the trifle!

blancmange. The rest of the soft blancmange flowed over the hole perfectly. You could not possibly tell that a spoonful was missing. The missing spoonful tasted delicious.

If it worked once, it would work many times—and Timothy was quite hungry. Squelch! Timothy's spoon finally dug into the jelly layer, which certainly was set hard. There was no hiding the jagged hole that remained. There was no hiding the disobedience of Timothy.

Miserably, Timothy made his way slowly upstairs to his room. How he wished he could have the last few minutes over again. He would certainly have left the trifle alone. But now, how upset he felt!

He did not have to wait long before he heard the key turn in the front door. Mum was talking excitedly to Teresa. The shopping expedition had gone well. Then there was silence. Then…

'Timothy! Come down here at once!'

It was a brief interview. Timothy was sent back up to his bedroom. Even though it was only four o'clock, he had to get straight into bed.

'I've got too much to get on with,' said a stern Mrs Bear. 'We'll wait to see what Dad has to say when he comes in from work.'

If anything, Timothy needed some time on his own to sort himself out. He was upset with himself. He had let his mum down, and at such a busy time. He was in danger of spoiling Teresa's baptism party.

Timothy had drawn his curtains, even though it was still the afternoon; the darkness suited his mood. But he really was sorry. How could he show that he really was sorry? Perhaps he would draw Teresa a picture. Although she was only young, she often smiled at his pictures. Yes! That's what he would do.

He put on his bedside lamp and got out of bed to find his paper and pencils. Then he stood still with surprise, paws outstretched, gazing at the far wall. The rays of light from the lamp were throwing up a shadow of himself on the wall, and it made the shape of a cross—maybe a shape of *the* cross.

Only the week before, at church, the vicar had been speaking about the cross of Jesus and how Jesus died in our place to put wrong things right. Did that mean, Timothy now wondered, even something like touching a trifle when you'd been told not to? As he settled to his drawing, Timothy felt strangely comforted.

Mr Bear's face was stern and serious when he came to deal with Timothy on his return from work. His face softened a little when he saw that Timothy had drawn his sister a lovely picture.

'Look, Dad,' said Timothy quietly, standing again in front of the bedside lamp. 'That's helping me as well.' Timothy was nodding at the cross-shaped shadow on the wall.

'We all need that to help us,' said Dad, equally quietly. 'Come down and make your peace with your mum and your sister.'

Early the next morning, Timothy helped Mum prepare a brand new trifle. When it was ready to go inside the fridge, Mum said, 'I don't think I need to tell you this time not to touch it.'

Timothy smiled. 'I'll only touch it when it's the proper time to eat it!'

The next day, at Teresa's baptism, the vicar invited Mr and Mrs Bear and Teresa's godparents to make the sign of the cross on her forehead. He explained that this is like an invisible badge; it shows that, when we are baptised, we are united with Christ and must not be ashamed to stand up for our faith in him.

The vicar also talked about how Jesus' death on the cross makes forgiveness possible. When the vicar spoke about the forgiveness that the cross of Jesus brings, Timothy remembered the shape on his bedroom wall and was thankful.

Activity

Make the shape of a cross out of paper or card. Decorate the cross and write on it the words, 'He died that we might be forgiven'. Keep it in your Baptism Box.

Prayer

Lord Jesus, you died that we might be forgiven. We are sorry for the wrong things we do and we thank you that you overcome them and everything that is evil. Amen

— Chapter 8 —

Promises, promises

In this story, Timothy breaks a promise. Then Mr Bear also breaks a promise. At the rehearsal for Teresa's baptism, the vicar talks about the promises made by parents, godparents and the church community to help the child follow Jesus. The story explores how easily young and old people can break their promises, wish they hadn't and determine to keep promises in future.

What the minister said

'Today we have all made promises. I wonder how good we are at keeping our word.'

Story preamble

Timothy breaks his promise… Dad breaks his promise… and they both end up promising to keep promises.

Bible verse

'I also remember the genuine faith of your mother Eunice. Your grandmother Lois had the same sort of faith, and I am sure that you have it as well.'
2 TIMOTHY 1:5

PROMISES, PROMISES

Sunday was going to be Teresa's special day—the day of her baptism and, as it happened, her birthday as well. In case Timothy should feel a bit left out, Dad had already decided that he and Timothy would have an outing on Saturday afternoon, the day before Teresa's baptism.

'We'll go to the Natural History Museum,' said Dad.

Timothy was delighted. He had become very keen on dinosaurs and understood that the museum had lots of buttons to press and films to see—as well as all their exhibits. He would also be able to add to his knowledge of shells.

'We'll have to be back in time to go to Teresa's baptism rehearsal at church in the evening,' Dad pointed out. The vicar wanted to be sure that the main characters taking part in Teresa's baptism were comfortable with what the service would involve, and so he had arranged for a rehearsal to take place the evening before.

By mid-morning on Saturday, Timothy felt bored. He and Mum had made the second trifle early that morning. Now Mum and Dad were both out in the garden, tidying up for the relatives who would be coming to celebrate the next day. Timothy had been left indoors to keep a listening ear in case his baby sister woke up from her sleep.

Everything seemed to centre around Teresa these days. Timothy plonked himself down on the settee in the lounge, and the springs made him bounce a little.

Timothy remembered that a few months ago he had bounced up and down on that very settee, fallen off and hurt his paw. Dad had made him promise never again to use the settee as a trampoline. It was one of several 'house rules' that Timothy had promised to keep. But surely, now he was older, he wouldn't fall off? He checked through the window to see that his parents were still busy in the garden. They were!

Timothy was surprised at how much steadier he was on his paws. He could jump up quite high today. He did wobble a little, but waving his paws soon corrected his balance.

He forgot about the shelf next to the settee, the shelf that held the precious vase that Auntie Sandra had given them for Christmas. Timothy's waving paw knocked the vase, and Timothy's wobble seemed to transfer to the vase.

The crash of the vase on the lounge floor coincided with Dad's return from the garden. Dad was through the door and into the lounge before Timothy had managed to stop bouncing.

'Timothy, you promised me...' began a stern Mr Bear.

The ringing of the telephone interrupted Timothy's telling-off. Dad went to answer it, and Timothy went to find a dustpan and brush.

As Timothy returned to the lounge with the dustpan and brush, he heard the end of Dad's telephone conversation. 'Oh, he won't mind,' he was saying. 'We can go to a museum any old time.'

Timothy couldn't believe his ears. 'Any old time?'

Dad came back smiling, tellings-off forgotten for the time being.

'That's a bit of luck!' Dad said. 'Uncle Chris has got a

spare ticket for the Bearchester United game this afternoon, and he wants me to go with him. I'm in the mood for a football match.'

'But you promised,' yelled Timothy Bear, stamping out of the lounge and upstairs to his bedroom.

It was a subdued Bear family that eventually gathered in the church that evening for Teresa's rehearsal, but the vicar was his usual cheerful self.

'Tomorrow,' he began, 'is a day for promises—family promises, godparent promises, church family promises. Promises are for keeping.'

The vicar encouraged Teresa's family and godparents to keep the promises they had made to help her learn all about Jesus and follow him in her life. He explained that it was up to the child's godparents and the church community to help Teresa follow a way of life that reflected goodness and light—and to share this light with others.

The vicar told everyone that this was why godparents and parents make the same promises on behalf of the child being baptised. Godparents promise to help the parents bring the child up in the Christian faith, with prayer and support. It is an important and responsible role.

The vicar looked kindly around the small group gathered in church. 'I wonder when we last broke a promise—and how we felt about it.'

That was the moment when Timothy and Dad caught each other's eye. After the rehearsal, Dad nodded that Timothy should come towards the porch. There, they hugged each other, Dad and cub.

'I'm so sorry I bounced on the settee,' said Timothy quietly.

'And I'm sorry I put football before you,' said Dad.

'It will never happen again,' they both said together.

'I promise,' they both said as one. And they both really meant it.

Activity

Draw one picture of the vase showing how it looked before it was broken. Then draw another picture showing how it looked after it had been smashed into pieces. Write a promise on your picture of the whole vase, and think about what might happen if that promise were broken. Place the pictures in your Baptism Box.

Prayer

Dear God, we thank you that you promise to love the world and everyone in it. We are sorry when we break our promises. Make us stronger to keep our promises in the future. Amen

Chapter 9

Light of Teresa's life

When Teresa was baptised, the vicar lit a large candle in the church. He also gave Mr and Mrs Bear a lighted candle at the end of the service, to remind them that Jesus is the light of the world and his light has come into Teresa's life. Timothy wants to help bring the light of Jesus into his little sister's life and does so by letting her hold on to his paw... and even by singing.

What the minister said

'You have received the light of Christ; walk in this light all the days of your life.'

Story preamble

Timothy comforts his baby sister at bath time... even sings to her... and helps her through her baptism.

Bible verse

Once again Jesus spoke to the people. This time he said, 'I am the light for the world! Follow me, and you won't be walking in the dark. You will have the light that gives life.'
JOHN 8:12

LIGHT OF TERESA'S LIFE

There were many times, after Teresa had been born, when Mum and Dad needed Timothy's help to look after their new little cub. Teresa took her time to get used to some of life's happenings. She cried quite a bit. Bath time was one of those happenings. She would yell in protest right from the beginning, as the water surrounded her body. Her fur would turn orange. It would take her many baths before she worked out how pleasant bathing could be.

In the early days, Timothy found that if he reached out his own paw to his sister's tiny paw, she would grip on to him and find some comfort. Her yells would lessen and sometimes her crying would cease altogether. So, while Mum and Dad made sure Teresa had a thorough washing, Timothy would be on 'paw duty', helping his sister at bath time.

'You're a real light of your sister's life!' Mum would exclaim.

Timothy also found that Teresa's tears sometimes stopped when he started singing to her. That was very strange, as you may know what a growler of a singer Timothy is. He would never be invited to join any choir! But somehow, in the times of her distress, Teresa found comfort in her brother's voice.

'The bear went over the mountain,' Timothy would sing three times, 'and what do you think he saw?' By then Teresa would have calmed down and Timothy would cheerfully—if tunelessly—conclude, 'The other side of the mountain!'

'You're a real light of your sister's life,' Mum would exclaim again. She was thrilled with the friendship growing between her two cubs.

Mum and Dad wondered how Teresa would respond to the water being poured over her at her baptism. Would it remind her of those bath times when she had shrieked and shrieked? Timothy was put on 'paw duty' once more. When the vicar was about to baptise Teresa, Timothy made sure he was in just the right place.

Those watching smiled when they saw Timothy offer his paw to his sister. By now, her grip was very tight. But there was not a single cry.

'I baptise you in the name of the Father, and of the Son, and of the Holy Spirit,' announced the vicar.

However, those watching could not hear what Timothy whispered in his sister's ear as the vicar said, 'Amen.'

'The other side of the mountain,' was what Timothy whispered!

Later that evening, back at home, Mr Bear lit Teresa's baptismal candle for the first time. It was a large candle, and the Bears planned to light it for a couple of hours on each anniversary of the day. When his maths was up to it, Timothy would be able to work out the number of years the candle would last.

This first evening, the godparents were saying how good Teresa had been in the church.

'Especially when the water was poured on her,' said one.

'Well,' replied Mrs Bear, 'I think her brother might have had a lot to do with that. He's a light of her life, you know.'

And Timothy, in the circle of light from the baptismal candle, modestly supposed he was.

Activity

Talk with a grown-up about ways in which you could bring light into the lives of people who are going through times of sadness. Place a tealight candle in your Baptism Box as a reminder about the things you thought of.

Prayer

Lord Jesus, you are the light of the world and you ask us to shine your light into our world. Help us to find ways to do just that. Amen

— Chapter 10 —

Serving others

Timothy remembers the time when he attended the induction of their new vicar. He thinks about how he can be of service to others when he helps Mrs Bradman. He then encourages his family to be part of church life as well.

What the minister said

'Go in the light and peace of Christ.'

Story preamble

Timothy remembers attending the induction of the new vicar... ministers to Mrs Bradman... and encourages his parents to minister as well.

Bible verse

But you are God's chosen and special people. You are a group of royal priests and a holy nation. God has brought you out of darkness into his marvellous light. Now you must tell all the wonderful things that he has done.

1 PETER 2:9

SERVING OTHERS

Timothy would sometimes tell Teresa a bedtime story to help her get to sleep. Sometimes his stories were based on his own life. Today, the day after her baptism, Timothy thought he would tell her about the vicar's induction.

Timothy was going to attend 'the induction' at the church—whatever that was! He'd never been to one before, and grown-ups can be bad at explaining things.

Timothy did know that there were going to be lots of refreshments. All the church people were going to be there. The Reverend Moody was the main one. He was going to be their new vicar, and the induction was especially for him. Apparently, it was quite a relief for everyone to have a new vicar.

'It's about time,' said Timothy's dad.

'Perhaps I won't have to do the flowers so often,' said his mum.

'I might stop visiting Mrs Bradman,' went on Dad. 'I'm so busy these days, and Reverend Moody might take her on.'

Timothy's mum and dad had been trying to keep an eye on Mrs Bradman, who lived a few houses away from them on their side of the road. She was quite elderly, getting towards 90 years old.

Timothy wondered what he could give up. Cubs' club, perhaps? Maybe he wouldn't bother to do so much Bible reading. After all, Reverend Moody must be able to do enough for two or three people.

It was good fun at the induction. Everyone came. There

was excitement in the air. The service was interesting, and even Timothy realised that the singing was special. Reverend Moody officially became their vicar. Then it was time for refreshments. Sausage rolls! Honey cakes! So many different kinds of crisps. Timothy was happy to be there a long time—he was one of the last to leave.

When they arrived home, Timothy's mum remembered Mrs Bradman's magazine. 'I've forgotten to pop it in to Mrs B,' she said. 'Be a good cub, Timothy, and take it round to her.'

Timothy took the magazine and set off. It wasn't far. Mrs Bradman was looking out of her window, as she often did. She tapped on the window and signalled to Timothy to wait for her to open the door.

'How kind of you!' she said. 'Please come in for a minute and tell me all about the service.'

It was nice indoors, and Mrs Bradman was full of interesting chatter. In the end, she said, 'I mustn't keep you too long, but I did cook a batch of flapjack this afternoon…'

'I could always phone home to let them know I'm staying a bit,' said quick-thinking Timothy.

'What a sensible cub you are,' replied Mrs Bradman. 'You really are ministering to me.'

Timothy had heard a lot about ministering at the induction, and had thought it was only something vicars did.

'Hello, Dad,' said Timothy over the phone. 'I won't be long. I'm ministering to Mrs Bradman.'

'You're doing what?' demanded Timothy's dad, in amazement. 'Oh, all right. Be home by seven.'

Mrs Bradman brought in the sticky flapjack. It was delicious. She went on talking about such interesting things—playing conkers, finding fossils in her garden, and the collection of coins she had. In a flash, the clock was striking a quarter to seven.

'Your visit has been a real ministry to me,' said Mrs Bradman. 'I haven't enjoyed myself so much in a long time.'

'It's been fun for me, too,' said Timothy, smiling and rubbing his tummy. 'I thought only people like Reverend Moody had a ministry.'

'You're just as good at it as I hope he'll be,' went on Mrs Bradman. 'Let's make you the Reverend Timothy Bear.'

Mrs Bradman took a piece of paper and folded it over several times. Then she fixed it with a paperclip round Timothy's neck.

'This is sometimes called a dog collar,' she said with a smile, 'but for you it's a bear collar!'

Of course, when he got home, Timothy had to explain. It was all great fun. His mum said, 'I'll carry on with the flowers. It's part of my ministry.'

Timothy's dad had something to say as well. 'Now that Reverend Timothy Bear has taken over Mrs Bradman, I'd better find someone else to visit.'

'Bless you, my parents,' said Timothy, in his best vicar's voice.

Activity

Ask a grown-up to help you make some simple cakes or biscuits. When they are cooked and cooled, wrap them in some pretty paper as a gift for someone close to you. Put a copy of the recipe, or a picture of the cakes, in your Baptism Box as a reminder that God asks us all to help one another.

Prayer

Lord Jesus, we thank you for all the people that serve you in your church. Help us to be your servants too. Amen

— Chapter 11 —

Pirates ahoy!

Everyone in church welcomes Teresa as a new member of the church. They applaud to show how pleased they are that she is now part of God's great family. Soon the summer holidays arrive, and Timothy Bear looks forward to time away with his family... and then discovers that a change of plan is not necessarily bad news.

What the minister said

'Teresa is now part of our family in Jesus. May she know the joy and happiness of what that means.'

Story preamble

The Bears can't go away on holiday... the church comes to the rescue... and Pirate Timothy 'shivers his timbers'.

Bible verses

A body is made up of many parts, and each of them has its own use. That's how it is with us. There are many of us, but we are each part of the body of Christ, as well as part of one another.
ROMANS 12:4–5

PIRATES AHOY!

It was quite a shock when Dad made the announcement. 'This year we're going to stay at home. We're not going away for a holiday this summer.'

Timothy remembered the lovely seaside holidays he and his family had enjoyed for the last couple of years. He loved the sea and sand, the rock pools and the pebbles. It was there that he had gained his great interest in shells. But why not this year?

Dad went on to explain that it wouldn't be so easy taking baby Teresa on holiday and, anyway, they had to be more careful about spending money. Timothy wondered what on earth he would do. How would he spend his time? What fun would he have?

In July, it was announced at church that there would be a holiday club in the mornings of the first week of the school holidays. Timothy would be just old enough to go.

'That's good,' said Mum. 'It will make up for us not going away.'

Timothy wasn't so sure. He would still miss the seaside, and he thought it might be too much like school. Anyway, Timothy's name was added to the list of those who would attend.

The day before holiday club was due to start, Claude's mother telephoned Mrs Bear in a lot of distress. Claude's family had only recently moved into Timothy's road, and now Claude's grandad had been taken into hospital. That meant all their holiday plans had to be changed.

'I wonder if there's room for Claude in holiday club,' said Mrs Bear. 'I'll phone the vicar.'

When the vicar heard the circumstances, it was arranged for Claude's name to be added to the list.

'You'll be able to look after Claude,' pointed out Mum to Timothy.

Again, Timothy wasn't so sure. Going to holiday club was one thing, but now he was supposed to look after someone he hardly knew.

'By the way,' went on Mum, 'you might find these helpful.'

She gave Timothy an eye patch on elastic and a red scarf with white dots all over it. She had read that the theme of the holiday club was going to be pirates. Timothy's hopes began to rise.

The church had been transformed so that it looked like a huge boat. 'Welcome to the Jolly Roger,' called out the vicar to the crowd of children and bears who had come.

It was great fun right from the start. They began all together in the main church. There were lots of shouts of 'Ah! Me hearties!' and 'Shiver me timbers!' and 'Pieces of eight!' There were songs to sing, fitness exercises to be done, live drama to be enjoyed and DVDs of Bible stories to be watched.

That first morning, the Jolly Roger pretended to come alongside Noah's ark.

Halfway through the morning, everyone was put into their age groups. Timothy found himself next to Claude. Their group was called the 'Mini Monsters', and they were to meet in the Small Hall.

'I know where that is,' said Timothy to Claude.

In the Small Hall, the Mini Monsters had refreshments and then found out more about Noah's ark. Next, there were animals to make and colour before adding them to the boat shape on the wall. Finally, they all made a cardboard parrot, like the ones that all pirates should have.

'We're going back to the Jolly Roger for the last ten minutes before your parents take you home,' announced the Mini Monsters' leader, who called herself Long John Sylvia.

Timothy could not believe that the whole morning had gone by so quickly. It had easily been as much fun as a morning on the beach. By Thursday afternoon, Timothy knew Claude well enough to ask Mrs Bear to invite him home. In actual fact, that week was the start of a firm friendship.

Claude said, 'I'm hearing those Bible stories for the first time. They're all new to me.'

Timothy got out his picture book of Bible stories and easily found the story of Noah's ark. Since the Noah's ark morning on Monday, the Jolly Roger had pretended to stop alongside Jonah when he was swallowed by a huge fish (Tuesday); it had also sailed next to the small boat in the storm on the Sea of Galilee, when Jesus woke up and calmed the waves (Wednesday). Timothy knew where to find those stories too, so he showed Claude.

On Thursday morning, the Jolly Roger came alongside another boat on the Sea of Galilee, when 153 fish were caught and Jesus cooked breakfast on the beach.

'It's as good as a seaside holiday,' chuckled Claude, and by now Timothy was in complete agreement. Neither of them could wait for next year's holiday club. And now that Teresa was baptised and officially part of the family of the church, Timothy knew it wouldn't be long before she too started to realise what fun church could be.

Activity

Make yourself something to do with pirates—an eye patch, a parrot, a treasure map or something else of your own choosing.

Put inside your Baptism Box something that makes you giggle or laugh. It might be a joke or a picture or something you have made.

Prayer

Lord Jesus, thank you for all the fun and laughter there is in our lives. Help us to enjoy sharing such times with others. Amen

— Chapter 12 —

If a job's worth doing...

Grandpa carves the shape of a scallop shell out of wood. It reminds Timothy of the shell that the vicar used for Teresa's baptism. He learns that worthwhile things often take a long time to happen, and ends up having a lovely surprise. Timothy's surprise is that Grandpa has been carving a wooden scallop shell shape for him as well.

What the minister said

'In baptism, God invites us on a lifelong journey. He is the way and he is its destination.'

Story preamble

Timothy spends time with Grandpa and learns that worthwhile things often take a long time to happen… and he ends up with a lovely surprise.

Bible verse

'I am the way, the truth, and the life!' Jesus answered. 'Without me, no one can go to the Father.'
JOHN 14:6

IF A JOB'S WORTH DOING…

Timothy Bear's grandpa has quite a few talents, and carpentry is certainly one of them. He can make wonderful things out of wood. Whenever he visits Grandma and Grandpa, Timothy loves to watch Grandpa at work in his shed in the garden. He stands as still as a statue, taking in all that Grandpa is doing.

Grandpa is slowly teaching Timothy to work with wood as well. At first, Timothy learned to hammer nails into wood, straight and firm. He found it harder learning to use a saw.

Grandpa has several projects on the go at the same time. Some months ago, he began working on a model of the church that the Bear family attends.

'In five years' time,' explained Grandpa, 'it's going to be 100 years since our church was opened. This will be my centenary gift.'

'Five years is such a long time!' responded Timothy.

'Well, there's a lot of work to be done, and I want to get it right. If a job's worth doing, it's worth doing well.'

On his most recent visit, Grandpa showed Timothy how the church was coming on. Timothy was impressed. He could already recognise the main shape of the church, and a roughly shaped spire was in place.

Grandpa was working on the spire, smoothing it and making it more pointed. He showed Timothy how to use the sandpaper, and then Timothy was given a small section of the spire to smooth down himself.

'How long did it take you to become a carpenter?' Timothy asked Grandpa. Grandpa smiled.

'I began like you with a hammer, saw and sandpaper, over 60 years ago, and I still learn new things about wood every time I work with it. Only this morning I chiselled too hard and broke the model I was making.'

Timothy wanted to see what had gone wrong. Grandpa had been carving the shape of a scallop shell out of wood.

'I'm making it for that sister of yours, as a reminder of her baptism. Do you remember, Timothy, how you found the vicar's shell when he couldn't remember where he'd put it?'

Timothy certainly did remember. Even though there was now a hole in the wooden shell, it was wonderfully smooth to hold in his paws. He thought how lucky Teresa would be to have it.

'Can't you patch it?' Timothy wanted to know. 'I'm sure Teresa wouldn't notice.'

'But we would both know, wouldn't we? And it wouldn't be the best I can do. No! I'll make a new one. If a job's worth doing, it's worth doing well.'

Grandpa and grandcub went back to work on the model of the church. Timothy worked very carefully. He didn't want to rub too hard and break the spire! He hoped that he would still be trying to be a better carpenter in 60 years' time.

'What made you want to be a carpenter in the first place?' was Timothy's next question. Again, Grandpa smiled.

'You and your curiosity!' said Grandpa patiently. 'I remember it had something to do with me being given the part of Joseph in the nativity play. The first scene was at Nazareth, and, as Joseph was a carpenter, I had to pretend to be making a manger out of planks of wood. So that Christmas I was given my first real tools.'

Timothy enjoyed the thought of Grandpa being Joseph. Last year, in the church nativity play, Timothy had been the king bringing gold to the baby Jesus.

Grandpa was still talking: 'Then it came to me that Jesus must have grown up to be a carpenter himself, so it helped me to find out more about him.'

'And how long did it take you to find out all about Jesus?' was Timothy's final question.

'Ah now,' said Grandpa, 'the longest life cannot even scratch the surface of finding out all there is to know about him.'

What a lot there was for Timothy to think about!

Two weeks later, Timothy had a great surprise. When Grandpa came round to present his wooden scallop shell to Teresa, he had made one to present to Timothy as well.

Activity

Find a shell, a piece of wood or a stone that you really like. Wonder about how old it is and where it comes from. Place it in your Baptism Box as a reminder of God's love.

Prayer

Lord Jesus, when we begin things, help us to see them through. Help us to go on learning new things about you all our lives. Amen

About the author

Brian Sears is a trained teacher with nearly 40 years' experience of primary education. He was head teacher at Yorke Mead School, Croxley Green, Hertfordshire from 1980 until his early retirement in 1997. Brian frequently leads church services by invitation, and has contributed to the Scripture Union Bible reading notes, *Snapshots*, for primary school-aged children. He has written three other books about Timothy Bear for Barnabas for Children.

Journal pages

Notes

Notes

Notes

Notes

Also by Brian Sears

Countdown to Christmas with Timothy Bear

24 five-minute read-aloud bedtime stories for Advent

For Timothy Bear, counting the days down to Christmas is full of excitement! At school there is the nativity play to get ready; at home there are decorations to put up, Christmas cards to write and tasty Christmas treats to prepare. It's no wonder Timothy sometimes finds himself daydreaming—floating through time and space, spinning but never dizzy, speeding but never frightened, until he lands with the slightest bump right in the middle of another adventure.

You, too, can count down the days to Christmas with Timothy Bear. All together there are 24 exciting read-aloud bedtime stories for the days of Advent. Each day there is also something to do to help you think about getting ready for Christmas, and a simple bedtime prayer.

ISBN 978 1 84101 725 9   £6.99
Available from your local Christian bookshop or direct from BRF: please visit brfonline.org.uk

Also from Barnabas for Children

Getting Ready for Baptism

A practical course preparing children for baptism

Richard Burge, Penny Fuller and Mary Hawes

Baptism is a very special moment in the Christian journey. It is a moment of awe and wonder, and of recognition that we are accepted by God and special in his sight.

Getting Ready for Baptism recognises that baptism can take place at any age and stage of life. Its aim is to deepen understanding of the biblical background to baptism for all involved and to explore what it means to be a child of God. With the emphasis on facilitating rather than a teacher-led approach, the material seeks to encourage all those involved in the sacrament, whether they are the candidate, the parent, godparent, friend, extended family member or member of the church community.

Part 1 explores the relationship between the candidate, parents and godparents, examines the place of discipleship for those taking part, considers the implications of baptism for the whole worshipping community, and places the emphasis on baptism being a step to belonging as well as a statement of belief. Part 2 offers three practical sessions: *Come to the party!*, *Enjoy the party!* and *Party on!*

ISBN 978 0 85746 019 6   £8.99
Available from your local Christian bookshop or direct from BRF: please visit brfonline.org.uk

Also from Barnabas for Children

My Baptism Journey

Activity Book

Richard Burge, Penny Fuller and Mary Hawes

This activity book accompanies the course book *Getting Ready for Baptism* and is intended for children to use at home to help them think about their baptism journey.

Children add their own thoughts in the spaces provided. They can write or draw as much or as little as they like. There are also fun tasks to complete, and space to stick in photographs of the baptism itself.

At the back of the book is a colour wheel to help children describe their thoughts and feelings. They are encouraged to choose a colour that feels right for them at that moment.

Written and developed as an ecumenical initiative between Methodist Children and Youth and the Church of England, with support from the United Reformed Church.

ISBN 978 0 85746 020 2   £3.99
Available from your local Christian bookshop or direct from BRF: please visit brfonline.org.uk

Also from Barnabas for Children

Through the Year with Who Let The Dads Out?

A year's worth of ideas for reaching out to dads and their preschool children

Mark Chester and Tony Sharp

This book provides everything you need to set up and run a Who Let The Dads Out? session!

There is a year's worth of session material for group leaders, including fresh ideas for themes and crafts, alongside musings on wider issues such as 'God slot, or not?', 'The long view: life after Who Let The Dads Out?' and 'The bacon butty: how do you make yours?'

ISBN 978 1 84101 727 3 £6.99
Available from your local Christian bookshop or direct from BRF: please visit brfonline.org.uk

Also from BRF

Parenting Children for a Life of Faith

Helping children meet and know God

Rachel Turner

Nurturing children in the Christian faith is a privilege given to all of us whose prime job it is to raise children. God's desire is that our parenting should guide each child to meet and know him, and to live with him every day through to eternity.

Parenting Children for a Life of Faith explores how the home can become the primary place in which children are nurtured into the reality of God's presence and love, equipped to access him themselves and encouraged to grow in a two-way relationship with him that will last a lifetime. The material explores:

- Discipling our children proactively
- Modelling the reality of being in a relationship with God
- Tying together truth and experience
- Connecting children to God's heart
- Implementing a plan

Each chapter includes true stories and questions to help us reflect on our own experience as we journey together with our children.

ISBN 978 1 84101 607 8   £7.99
Available from your local Christian bookshop or direct from BRF: please visit brfonline.org.uk

Also from BRF

Parenting Children for a Life of Purpose

Empowering children to become who they are called to be

Rachel Turner

'Too long we have stood apart as a church and looked at children and teens and said, "We love you, we value you, but we don't need you."'

Our churches have the power to establish a community of purpose that all people participate in. They can be the places where children feel most powerful, most seen, most discipled and most released. We can be the church that God designed. *Parenting Children for a Life of Purpose* is a practical and tested handbook exploring the possibilities for helping children to discover the specific gifts for whatever God is calling them to be, and showing how parents might partner with churches to enable children to discover their true identity and purpose in life and walk alongside them on the journey.

Addressing issues of identity, relationship, purpose, power, love, calling and response, each chapter includes true stories and questions to help us to reflect on our own experiences.

ISBN 978 0 85746 163 6   £7.99
Available from your local Christian bookshop or direct from BRF: please visit brfonline.org.uk

Enjoyed this book?

Write a review—we'd love to hear what you think.
Email: reviews@brf.org.uk

Keep up to date—receive details of our new books as they happen. Sign up for email news and select your interest groups at:
www.brfonline.org.uk/findoutmore/

Follow us on Twitter @brfonline

By post—to receive new title information by post (UK only), complete the form below and post to: BRF Mailing Lists, 15 The Chambers, Vineyard, Abingdon, Oxfordshire, OX14 3FE

Your Details
Name _____
Address _____
_____
Town/City _____ Post Code _____
Email _____

Your Interest Groups (*Please tick as appropriate)
☐ Advent/Lent ☐ Messy Church
☐ Bible Reading & Study ☐ Pastoral
☐ Children's Books ☐ Prayer & Spirituality
☐ Discipleship ☐ Resources for Children's Church
☐ Leadership ☐ Resources for Schools

Support your local bookshop
Ask about their new title information schemes.